If you know what it is like
when friends run away
and one person is left alone and
in trouble,
then you will be astonished
to read about...

Text by Lois Rock
Copyright © 1996 Lion Publishing
Illustrations copyright © 1996 Roger Langton

The author asserts the moral right
to be identified as the author of this work

Published by
**Lion Publishing plc**
Sandy Lane West, Oxford, England
ISBN 0 7459 3111 1
**Lion Publishing**
4050 Lee Vance View, Colorado Springs, CO 80918, USA
ISBN 0 7459 3111 1
**Albatross Books Pty Ltd**
PO Box 320, Sutherland, NSW 2232, Australia
ISBN 0 7324 0971 3

First edition 1996
10 9 8 7 6 5 4 3 2 1 0

A catalogue record for this book is available
from the British Library

Library of Congress CIP data applied for

Printed and bound in Singapore

**This retelling is based on the stories
of Jesus' life in the Bible.**

# Jesus All Alone

Retold by Lois Rock
Illustrations by Roger Langton

A LION BOOK

It was a day in spring, long ago. Lots of people were travelling to Jerusalem for a special festival.

When they heard that Jesus was coming too, there was great excitement.

"Jesus is coming! Jesus is coming!"
"I want to see!"

"I'm going to wave!"
"Let's make a carpet for his donkey to walk on—like they do for kings."

"I've spoken to him," some said. "He was kind to me. He made me feel special. He's my best friend."

At that moment, it seemed that everyone in the world wanted to be friends with Jesus. There were smiling crowds all around.

But Jesus had always had enemies. Some people didn't like the way he talked about God: he said God welcomed people. What nonsense!

"God doesn't want bad people as friends!" they argued. "God wants people who keep the rules. We know the rules. We teach the rules." They wanted to get rid of Jesus.

It was one of Jesus' close friends who let
him down: Judas Iscariot.

Judas told Jesus' enemies where they could find him.

That evening, Jesus went to an olive grove to pray. Eleven of his close friends were with him.

Then there was a clatter: Judas led some armed men to take Jesus to his enemies.

Jesus did not try to run. He did not try to fight.

But he must have felt sad when his friends ran away, afraid.

Jesus was dragged before his enemies. They tried to prove he had done wrong things. They told lies about him to get him into trouble.

Jesus didn't argue or shout back.

The soldiers who were told to guard Jesus were used to bullying their prisoners.

They teased him and hit him. Jesus didn't get angry.

The ruler of the country, Pontius Pilate, could see that Jesus had done no wrong. "I always set a prisoner free at the time of this special festival," he said to himself. "I'll ask the crowds if they want me to set Jesus free."

But Jesus' enemies had told the crowds what to say: "Kill him! Crucify him!"

Jesus was all alone. None of his friends dared come near. They were too scared.

Jesus let it happen: all the bad things, all the cruel things, all the unkind things. His enemies put him to death. They nailed him to a cross of wood.

Before he died, Jesus said a prayer to God:

"Father, forgive them. They don't know what they are doing." Jesus loved everyone to the very end.

# A Christian prayer

Dear God,
You sent Jesus to show us
how much you love people.
He forgave the friends
who ran away.
He forgave the people
who hurt him.
Thank you for your love.
Thank you for your forgiveness.
Amen.